Real People

Harriet Tubman

By Philip Abraham

Welcome Books

Children's Press®
A Division of Scholastic Inc.
New York / Toronto / London / Auckland / Sydney
Mexico City / New Delhi / Hong Kong
Danbury, Connecticut

Photo Credits: Cover, pp. 5, 7, 9, 11, 13, 17, 21 © Hulton/Archive by Getty Images; pp. 15, 19 © Photographs and Prints Division, Schomburg Center for Research in Black Culture, The New York Public Library, Astor, Lenox and Tilden Foundations

Contributing Editor: Jennifer Silate
Book Design: Christopher Logan

Library of Congress Cataloging-in-Publication Data

Abraham, Philip, 1970–
    Harriet Tubman / by Philip Abraham.
        p. cm. — (Real people)
    Includes bibliographical references and index.
       Summary: A brief introduction to the life of Harriet Tubman, who spent her childhood in slavery and later worked to help other slaves escape north to freedom through the Underground Railroad.
       ISBN 0-516-23953-8 (lib. bdg.) — ISBN 0-516-23604-0 (pbk.)
    1. Tubman, Harriet, 1820?–1913—Juvenile literature. 2. Slaves—United States—Biography—Juvenile literature. 3. African American women—Biography—Juvenile literature. 4. Underground railroad—Juvenile literature. [1. Tubman, Harriet, 1820?–1913. 2. Slaves. 3. African Americans—Biography. 4. Women—Biography. 5. Underground railroad.] I. Title. II. Real people (Children's Press)

E444.T82 .A58 2002
973.7'115—dc21   2001042360

Contents

Meet Harriet Tubman.

She was born in **Maryland** around 1820.

At that time, some states allowed people to own **slaves**.

Harriet was a slave.

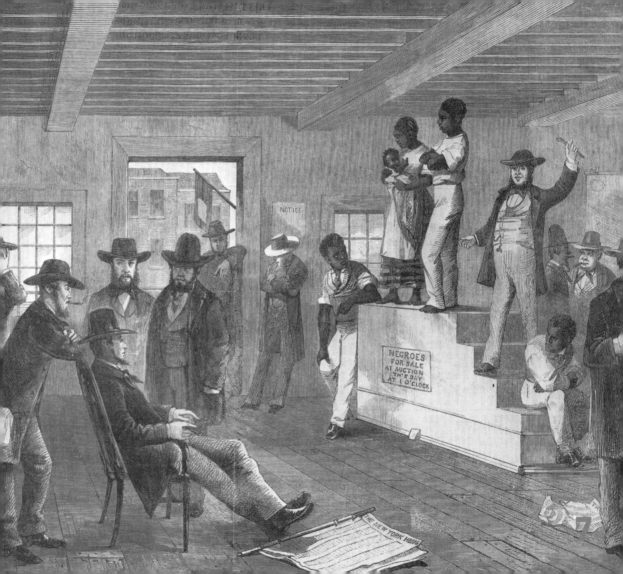

NEGROES
FOR SALE
AT AUCTION
TH'S DAY
AT 1 O'CLOCK

THE NEW YORK HERALD

Slaves had to work very hard.

Most slaves were treated badly.

Slave families often shared small houses.

In 1849, Harriet ran away from Maryland.

She went to **Pennsylvania**.

Pennsylvania did not allow people to own slaves.

Now, Harriet was **free**.

She helped other slaves become free, too.

She led them to the Northern states where **slavery** was not allowed.

Harriet helped about 300 slaves become free.

In 1861, the **Civil War** was fought in the United States.

Harriet worked as a nurse to help **soldiers** from the Northern states.

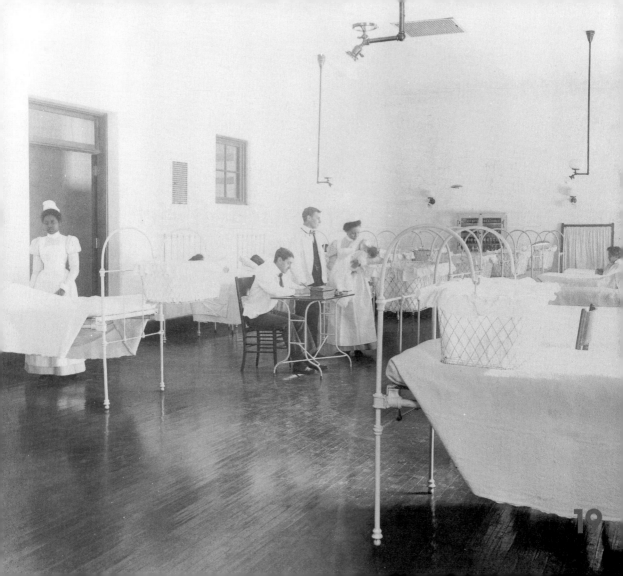

Harriet Tubman helped many people.

She was a great American.

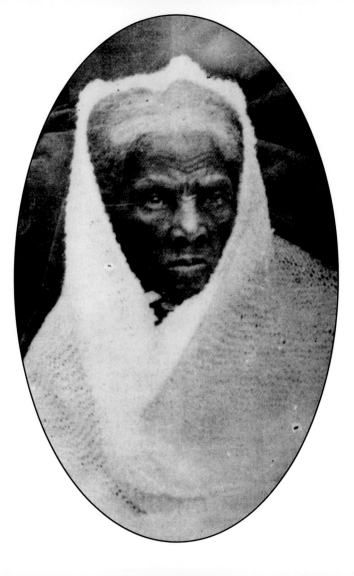

New Words

Civil War (**sihv**-uhl **wor**) a war between the Northern and Southern states of the United States from 1861 to 1865

free (**free**) not under someone else's control or rule

Maryland (**mair**-uh-luhnd) one of the Southern states of the United States

Pennsylvania (pehn-suhl-**vay**-nyuh) one of the Northern states of the United States

slavery (**slay**-vuhr-ee) the custom of owning people and forcing them to work

slaves (**slayvz**) people who are owned by other people and work for them

soldiers (**sohl**-juhrz) people who serve in an army

To Find Out More

Books
A Picture Book of Harriet Tubman
by David A. Adler
Holiday House

Escape North!: The Story of Harriet Tubman
by Monica Kulling
Random House

Web Site
Harriet Tubman and the Underground Railroad
http://www2.lhric.org/pocantico/tubman/tubman.html
This site was created by a second-grade class. It has fun puzzles, a
timeline, and other information about Harriet Tubman.

Index

About the Author

Philip Abraham is a freelance writer. He works in New York City.

Reading Consultants

Kris Flynn, Coordinator, Small School District Literacy, The San Diego County Office of Education

Shelly Forys, Certified Reading Recovery Specialist, W.J. Zahnow Elementary School, Waterloo, IL

Sue McAdams, Former President of the North Texas Reading Council of the IRA, and Early Literary Consultant, Dallas, TX